A Train's Day

by Betsy Rathburn
Illustrated by Christos Skaltsas

BLASTOFF!
MISSIONS

BELLWETHER MEDIA
MINNEAPOLIS, MN

Blastoff! Missions takes you on a learning adventure! Colorful illustrations and exciting narratives highlight cool facts about our world and beyond. Read the mission goals and follow the narrative to gain knowledge, build reading skills, and have fun!

Traditional Nonfiction

Narrative Nonfiction

Blastoff! Universe

MISSION GOALS

> FIND YOUR SIGHT WORDS IN THE BOOK.

> LEARN ABOUT WHAT DIFFERENT TRAIN CARS CARRY.

> LEARN ABOUT THE PEOPLE THAT WORK ON TRAINS.

This edition first published in 2024 by Bellwether Media, Inc.

No part of this publication may be reproduced in whole or in part without written permission of the publisher. For information regarding permission, write to Bellwether Media, Inc., Attention: Permissions Department, 6012 Blue Circle Drive, Minnetonka, MN 55343.

Library of Congress Cataloging-in-Publication Data

Names: Rathburn, Betsy, author.
Title: A train's day / by Betsy Rathburn.
Other titles: Blastoff! missions. Machines at work.
Description: Minneapolis, MN : Bellwether Media, Inc., 2024. | Series: Blastoff! Missions: Machines at work | Includes bibliographical references and index. | Audience: Ages 5-8 | Audience: Grades 2-3 | Summary: "Vibrant illustrations accompany information about the daily activities of a freight train. The narrative nonfiction text is intended for students in kindergarten through third grade." -- Provided by publisher.
Identifiers: LCCN 2023014197 (print) | LCCN 2023014198 (ebook) | ISBN 9798886873894 (library binding) | ISBN 9798886875270 (paperback) | ISBN 9798886875775 (ebook)
Subjects: LCSH: Railroad trains--Juvenile literature. | CYAC: Railroad trains. | LCGFT: Instructional and educational works.
Classification: LCC TF148 .T775 2024 (print) | LCC TF148 (ebook) | DDC 625.2--dc23/eng/20230330
LC record available at https://lccn.loc.gov/2023014197
LC ebook record available at https://lccn.loc.gov/2023014198

Text copyright © 2024 by Bellwether Media, Inc. BLASTOFF! MISSIONS and associated logos are trademarks and/or registered trademarks of Bellwether Media, Inc.

Editor: Christina Leaf   Designer: Andrea Schneider

Printed in the United States of America, North Mankato, MN.

This is **Blastoff Jimmy!** He is here to help you on your mission and share fun facts along the way!

Table of Contents

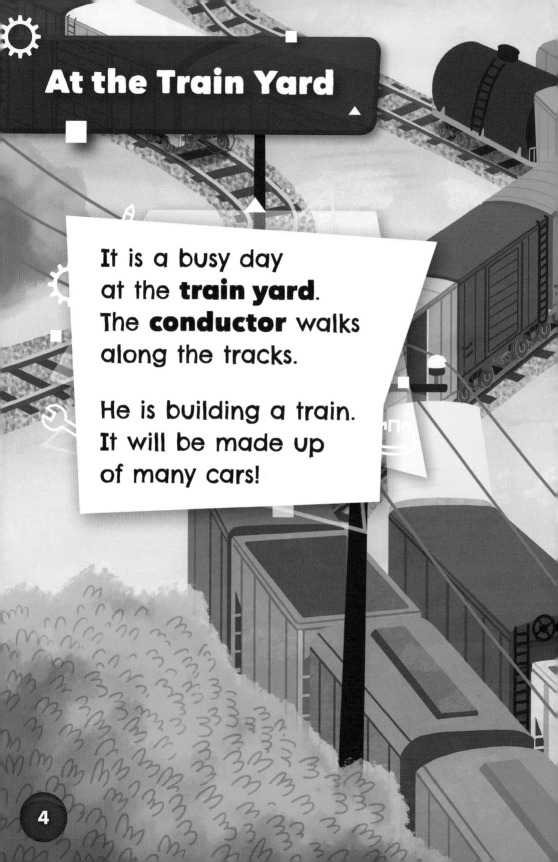

At the Train Yard

It is a busy day at the **train yard**. The **conductor** walks along the tracks.

He is building a train. It will be made up of many cars!

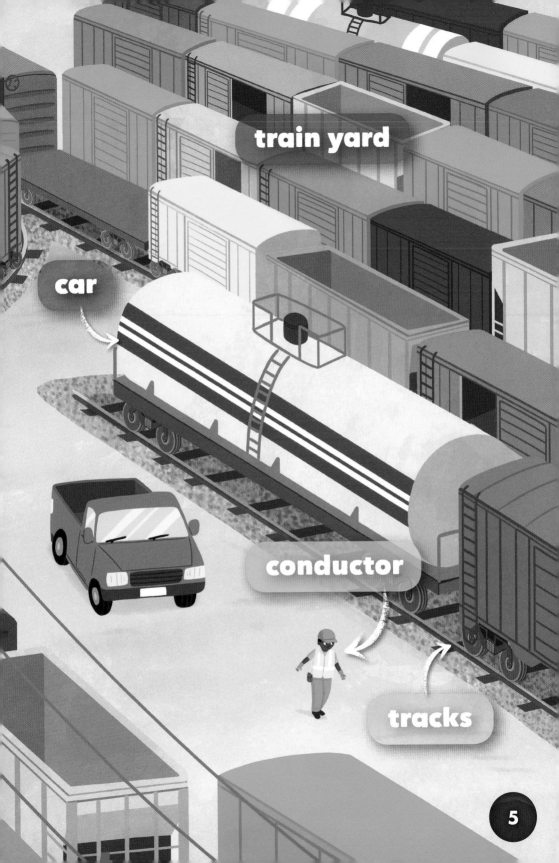

train yard

car

conductor

tracks

5

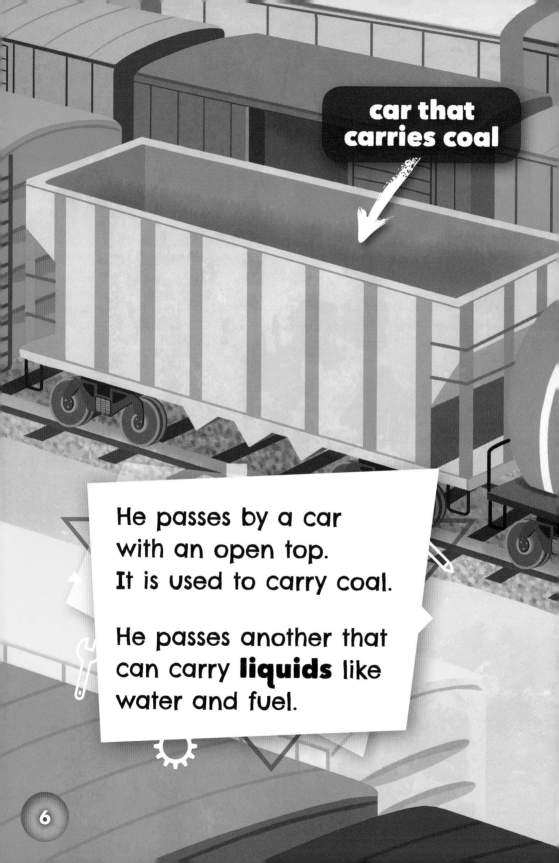

car that
carries coal

He passes by a car
with an open top.
It is used to carry coal.

He passes another that
can carry **liquids** like
water and fuel.

6

► **JIMMY SAYS** ◄
Most coal cars can carry over 200,000 pounds (90,718 kilograms) of coal!

car that carries liquids

The conductor chooses an empty **boxcar** to connect to the **locomotive**. Then he adds many more boxcars.

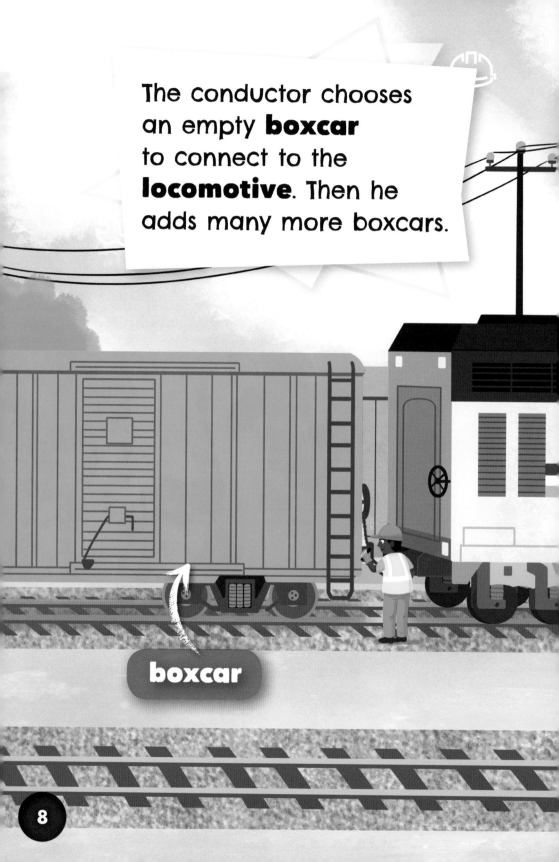

boxcar

locomotive

The boxcars will carry boxes of goods.

Finally, the last boxcar is connected. There are nearly 100!

The conductor checks the train for safety. It is ready to go!

On the Way

engineer

The **engineer** drives the train out of the train yard.

▶ **JIMMY SAYS** ◀

Trains have speed limits, too! Trains that carry goods are usually limited to 60 miles (97 kilometers) per hour.

The train follows the tracks slowly at first. Then it picks up speed!

Another train is coming.
This one carries people.

A **switch** will help!
It moves the tracks
to let the train
change paths.

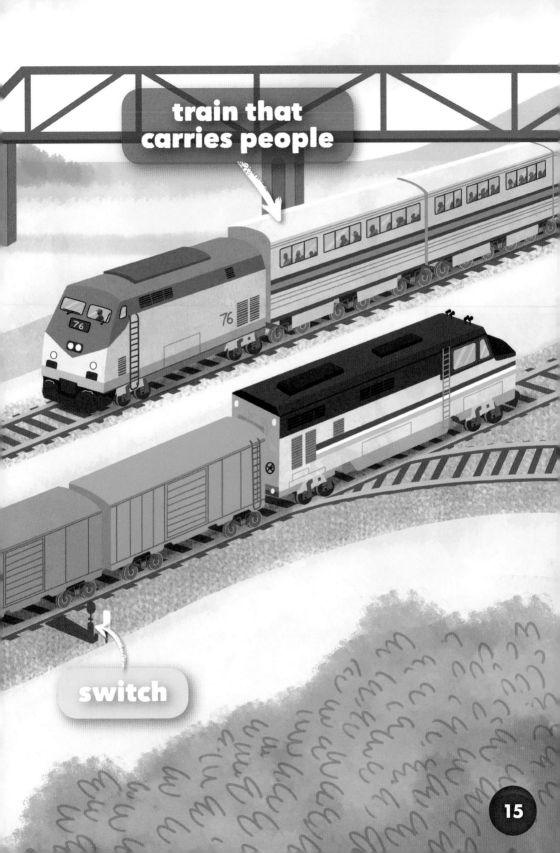

train that carries people

switch

15

Air brakes help the train slow down as it pulls into the **freight station**.

A worker drives a **forklift** up to the first boxcar once the train has stopped. She loads the boxcar with goods.

W. M.
27473

freight station

forklift

17

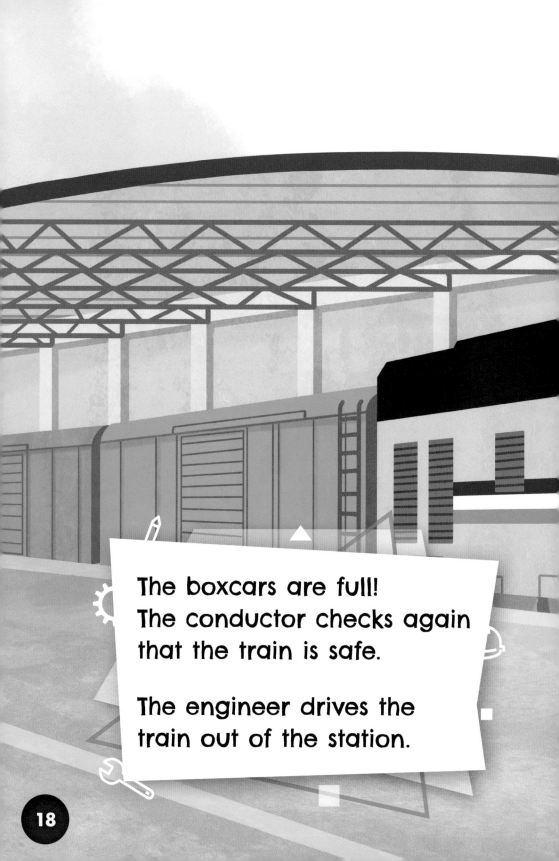

The boxcars are full!
The conductor checks again
that the train is safe.

The engineer drives the
train out of the station.

The train arrives at the next station. Workers unload the goods from the boxcars onto trucks.

The empty train will carry another load tomorrow!

truck

Train Jobs

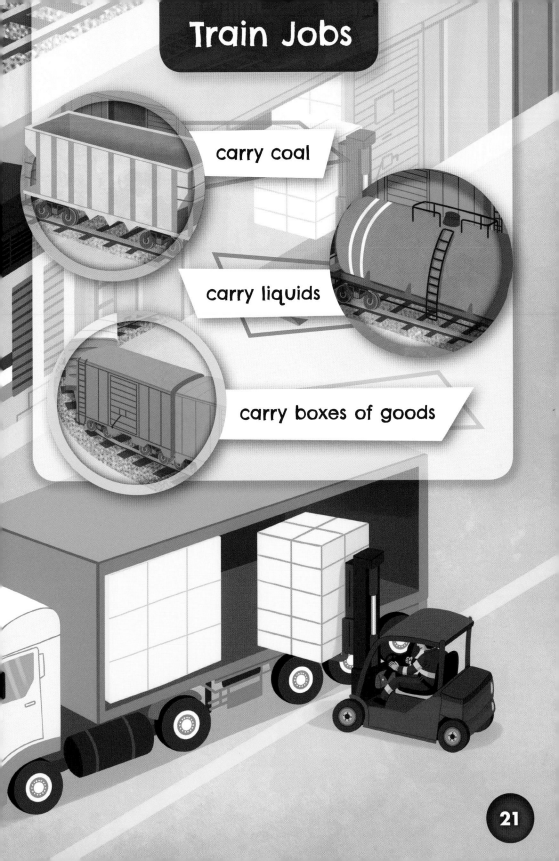

carry coal

carry liquids

carry boxes of goods

Glossary

air brakes–brakes that use air to stop wheels from turning

boxcar–an enclosed train car used to carry boxes of goods

conductor–a person who makes sure trains are put together and loaded safely, and keeps them on time

engineer–a person who drives a train

forklift–a machine used to lift heavy items

freight station–a place where trains stop to pick up and drop off goods

liquids–materials that can flow like water

locomotive–the part of a train that gives it power to move

switch–a part of a railroad track that can be moved to help trains change directions

train yard–a place where trains are built, loaded, and unloaded

To Learn More

AT THE LIBRARY

DK. *Eyewitness Train: Discover the Story of the Railroads.* New York, N.Y.: DK Children, 2022.

Duling, Kaitlyn. *Trains.* Minneapolis, Minn.: Bellwether Media, 2023.

Spray, Sally. *Awesome Engineering: Trains, Planes, and Ships.* North Mankato, Minn.: Capstone, 2018.

ON THE WEB

FACTSURFER

Factsurfer.com gives you a safe, fun way to find more information.

1. Go to www.factsurfer.com.

2. Enter "trains" into the search box and click 🔍.

3. Select your book cover to see a list of related content.

BEYOND THE MISSION

> THINK ABOUT THE TRAINS YOU HAVE SEEN. WHICH WAS THE LONGEST?

> WHAT FACT FROM THE BOOK DO YOU THINK IS THE MOST INTERESTING?

> DRAW YOUR OWN TRAIN AND TRACKS. WHERE DO THE TRACKS GO? WHAT DOES THE TRAIN CARRY?

Index